MOVING FORWARD

A Guide to Finding Peace and Yourself With or Without Reconciliation

KENDALL L. WILLIAMS

Copyright © 2025 Kendall L. Williams

All rights reserved. No part of this publication may be reproduced, stored or transmitted in any form or by any means, electronic, mechanical, photocopying, recording, scanning, or otherwise without written permission from the publisher. It is illegal to copy this book, post it to a website, or distribute it by any other means without permission.

BEFORE YOU BEGIN

Let me be crystal clear to anyone who may misunderstand the intent of this book, so no one thinks my intention is to push "non-reconciliation"! This book is not about giving up on reconciliation with your child—it's about finding some peace whether reconciliation happens or not and to make sure you don't lose yourself or who you have fought so hard to become, even if and when there is reconciliation. This book is also for those who have made the choice to NOT reconcile as well.

I need some of you to clearly understand that choosing to move forward doesn't mean you don't love your child anymore, it doesn't mean that you are abandoning your child, it just means that you cannot continue to stay stuck or stagnant. because time waits for no man nor woman.

Some of you didn't choose this distance—it was forced on you for reasons unknown and let's be honest; some reasons are very much known and you have to own that and take accountability for whatever that may be. But the need some of you have and the desperation seeking conciliation with your child that could happen at some point, must never come at the sacrifice of yourself. Accountability, forgiveness, boundaries and respect must be mutual. But if you've already taken ownership of your part, if and when it was warranted, you don't have to keep proving yourself to your child who keeps trying to force accountability on you. You are also not responsible for constantly validating their feelings and emotions when that same energy is not reciprocated from them as it relates to your feelings and emotions, then all this becomes emotional manipulation and abuse.

Some of you chose distance and are not seeking reconciliation right now. You choose for your own reasons, like me. Because distance for my own mental and physical wellbeing, was far more important than my proximity to my son right now.

Wherever you are as it relates to your estrangement journey, and rather you do or do not want reconciliation, this book is for you. It's for you to make a decision to move forward with or without reconciliation and to find or have peace in the process!

DEDICATIONS

To every parent who has cried in silence,
who has been judged without being understood,
who has carried love and heartbreak daily for children you have loved with everything in you.

To the mothers who have been silenced, shamed, or discarded—
yet still refuse to stay broken.

To the fathers who have carried love in one hand and pain in the other and remain silent because society tells you, you can't show your emotions even when you are hurting too.

This book is for you.
For your strength.
For your healing.
For your peace.

May these words remind you that you are not alone, that your worth was never tied to your child's choice to be estranged, not to the abuse and not to their choices,
and that reconciliation or not—
you are still worthy and a damn good parent.

TABLE OF CONTENTS

INTRODUCTION 1

CHAPTER 1 3
The Finality We Don't Want to Face

CHAPTER 2 13
Living Without Reconciliation And Without Guilt

CHAPTER 3 23
Releasing the Need for Their Approval

CHAPTER 4 35
Protecting Your Peace (Peace is the Boundary You Shouldn't Allow Anyone to Cross)

CHAPTER 5 45
Choosing Not to Reconcile

CHAPTER 6 55
Blood Doesn't Always Guarantee Love

CHAPTER 7 59
Reclaiming Joy (Finding Joy in the Life You Still Have)

CHAPTER 8 67
Writing a New Chapter for Yourself (Reclaiming Your Identity)

CHAPTER 9 77
Navigating Reconciliation if Your Child Returns

CHAPTER 10 79
Grandparents Bring It In

CLOSING 87
Your Peace Is Sacred

ACKNOWLEDGMENTS 89

INTRODUCTION

This book is for you if you've been carrying the weight of estrangement. It's for the parents who are tired of over-explaining, tired of sacrificing their sanity, tired of waiting for someone else to choose them or come running back to you. It's for those of you that are ready to move forward with or without reconciliation.

Whether the distance was chosen by them—or by you—this book is for you. My hope is to give you the permission and tools to move forward in peace—whether reconciliation comes or not.

I encourage you to read this with an open heart and an open mind.

There was a moment when I realized that no matter how much I wanted a great relationship with my youngest son or how much I often think of reconciliation, it could not come at the cost of myself. I had already apologized for anything he felt I did to hurt him, I had already allowed way too much disrespect, I had already allowed him to speak ill of me, defame and disparage my character to others, say the most disrespectful things to me, and I forgave him and would pick right back up where we left off as if it never happened. I had already heard every false narrative he created about me and overlooked it, already bent, already broke myself, already carried more weight than one heart should and continuously tried to fix things I did not break in the first place.

Moving Forward

What I realized is; my son is at war with himself for quite some time, it was time for me to exit the war and I desperately needed peace to save my own life. I chose estrangement with a heavy heart and I feel some of that pain every day. I realized that I deserve happiness, joy, love, respect and to live my life for me, even if reconciliation never comes. And if reconciliation ever does happen, it has to come with mutual accountability, his healing and changed behavior. Because it is not always the parent's responsibility to fix the relationship contrary to what society keeps shoving down our throats.

CHAPTER 1

The Finality We Don't Want to Face (When Hope Holds You Hostage)

Parents often feel like estrangement means finality—and in some cases, truthfully, it is. Finality and closure arrives in different ways. For some parents, it's the silence after too many unanswered calls or not having closure as to why. For others, it's the disrespect or even hearing the words 'I'm done.' And sometimes, it's just your own heart telling you the truth, we don't want to acknowledge—that continuing to wait for this reconciliation or for your child to come running back to you, is doing more harm than good. Finality and closure doesn't always come from them; sometimes it has to come from us.

There's a part of us that still wants reconciliation and have hope that it will happen! Estrangement is being called a "Movement" by some of the adult kids yet has no clear goal in mind as to the purpose of this "movement". Because movements normally have a goal in mind and the only movement this reminds me of is a bowel movement. But you still hold out with hope. But here's the truth I wish someone had told me sooner: sometimes reconciliation doesn't come—not because you're unworthy, not because you failed, but because the other person refuses to meet you halfway and sometimes

Moving Forward

that hope you have for reconciliation, needs to turn into your logical reality.

But you think maybe—just maybe—today will be the day your adult child calls and says, "I'm sorry. I miss you. Let's start over."

But sometimes being hopeful can be heavy and mentally exhausting.

Keep Living While You Wait

There is no reason to stay stagnant while you wait to reconcile with your child. You can keep living. You can keep laughing. You can find joy again. Some of you don't want to hear that, but it's the truth. Too many parents sit in heartbreak, sink deeper into depression, and stay stuck in mourning because they believe that showing joy means they don't love their child anymore. But that's a lie. In some cases, I honestly believe some of you want to stay in the space of being stagnant, you want to stay stuck in depression and heartbreak because if you choose the opposite, I think some of you feel guilt or feel like that will change things.

Let me repeat, moving forward doesn't erase your love for your child and you are not abandoning them. Besides how do you abandon someone who abandoned you first? Staying in pain doesn't prove anything except that you've abandoned yourself. Some of you hold on to the fantasy that if you look sad enough, if you show how broken you are, maybe your child will come back out of pity. But pity doesn't create reconciliation. And truthfully, most of them are out living their lives, not thinking about how heartbroken you feel.

You don't get them back by sacrificing yourself. You don't get reconciliation by staying miserable. You get your power

Moving Forward

back by getting up, choosing joy, peace, and proving to yourself that you can keep living whether they return or not.

Personal Story

I never thought my youngest son and I would be here. It's not something I wanted even when things have been toxic in the past. There's normally this cool off period when he falls back for a few days, weeks or months after HE has said nasty things to me. But not this time. No temporary cool-off was going to work for me after this last experience with him. It made me realize he was at war with himself and it was no longer my responsibility to be a POW. So I chose to escape and I have found this sense of peace that I am not willing to have disturbed until he does the healing work he needs to do and that is not contingent upon me.

But I too see finality as a kind of grief all its own. It's not the grief of a funeral, where the world acknowledges your loss and sends flowers. It's the grief of mourning the end of a relationship with someone you have loved unconditionally while the person is still alive.

And while people love to say, "There's always hope", hope can become a prison if it's tied to something outside of your control.

The Cost of Waiting

Waiting feels like you are never giving up and I'm not saying you should. But waiting also drains your spirit. It keeps you second-guessing yourself. Many of us were taught that a good parent never gives up, especially moms, but holding on at any cost isn't healthy—it's self-destruction and takes a very harmful toll on your mental wellbeing and sometimes physical being. I

Moving Forward

need moms to know that loving your child doesn't mean you abandon yourself. Courage is choosing peace even when it looks like letting go. You know that peace over proximity I talk about all of the time.

Let's Talk Healthy Hope vs. Toxic Hope

Hope can sustain you or suffocate you. Toxic hope keeps you in the cycle of: if I keep giving in, they'll come back. If I walk on eggshells, they won't get mad with me. If I tolerate their abuse or agree to their false narratives about me, they will reconcile with me. Some of you are sitting around waiting or accepting these scraps just because you are hoping your child will come back and that is not healthy.

Healthy hope says: "I have done my part. I have acknowledged or have been accountable for where I was wrong, I won't keep being a punching bag and I will set boundaries and if that is not good enough for us to work toward reconciliation, I release you with love because I will not continue carrying what isn't mine to carry, and I choose peace while leaving the door open to reconciliation."

- **Healthy hope** says: "I'm open to reconciliation, but I will live fully in the meantime."
- **Toxic hope** says: "I will put my life on hold until they come back."

When hope becomes toxic, it steals your present. It keeps you in a holding pattern, waiting for someone else's decision to determine your peace.

Moving Forward

Facing the Fear

The thought of never reconciling is terrifying for most parents. I totally get it. You think:

- *What will people think of me?*
- *What if they tell my grandchildren lies about me?*
- *What if I die and we're still not speaking?*

The truth? Those fears are valid. But they're also the very chains that keep you bound. Facing the fear—naming it—is the first step toward loosening its grip.

JOURNAL PROMPTS

If my relationship with my child never returns, what feelings come up for me right now?

_____
_____
_____
_____
_____
_____
_____
_____
_____
_____
_____
_____
_____
_____
_____
_____
_____
_____

Where in my life am I putting my peace on hold, waiting for someone else to make the first move or return?

What has been holding me back from letting go after so much time has passed?

"Peace begins the moment you stop waiting at a closed door and acknowledge the truth."

CHAPTER 2

Living Without Reconciliation And Without Guilt

Some of you will decide that reconciliation is not for you. That choice can be very painful. Because in most cases, who wants to be estranged from a child they love? This isn't a decision we came to overnight. This decision was absolutely arduous and came after years of trying, apologizing, forgiving, tolerating abuse, bending, and breaking and only at our expense.

At some point you realize: continuing to chase reconciliation was costing you your peace, your health, your joy. Choosing non-reconciliation is not failure. It is a boundary you're setting if you've been dealing with abuse, and it a decision that you are not going to stay stagnant desperately seeking reconciliation.

What I need you to know is this: you do not have to feel guilty for walking away. Society has programmed moms to always feel guilty for choosing what's best for us, especially as it relates to our kids. Guilt and judgmental people will constantly be that voice whispering in your ear that you're a "bad parent" if you stop trying, but that's a lie rooted in old thinking and expectations solely placed on mothers and I don't know about you, but I'm no longer subscribing to that

Moving Forward

unhealthy bullshit. Besides we have literally already given everything we had to give. Hell some of us have even given one of our kidneys. Protecting yourself is not abandoning your child, it's for your survival.

Not saying it is easy in most cases, but living without reconciliation means creating a life you can enjoy guilt-free. You can travel, laugh, fall in love with your partner or hell yourself, find some new hobbies, build or join a support community, and embrace peace without explanation. You can still love your child, but you don't have to set yourself on fire to prove it. Love can exist from a distance.

And be prepared for some of them to have the audacity to call you selfish when you stop chasing, stop waiting and start living for you. Some of them or outsiders will try to manipulate you with guilt. But here's the truth: most of our kids are living their lives without a second thought about yours. If they're free to live, so are you! You are allowed to keep loving and living life on your terms.

Reconciliation is always the hope. But not if it means being disrespected again and again. Detachment can also be a conscious choice: distance over disrespect. If you've already carried accountability, you don't have to keep proving yourself. But often making this decision without guilt is the most difficult part.

But detachment is also often misunderstood. People may see it as giving up, or abandoning their child, but it's not. Afterall, in most cases haven't most of them detached from parents already? Detachment, or moving forward does not equal you no longer loving your child or rejection—it's actually about your protection.

Moving Forward

Finally detaching if that is where you are on your journey, says: 'I love you, but I won't let your emotional abuse or your emotional manipulation, nor your choices destroy me.' Detachment isn't abandonment—it's survival and doing so without the emotional guilt that comes with it.

Distance is sometimes the only way to honor yourself. When disrespect, mental abuse, emotional abuse or financial or physical abuse becomes constant, detachment is necessary. Some parents reach a point where reconciliation isn't healthy, safe, or even desired. And that's okay. Refusing reconciliation is not the absence of love—it is the presence of self-preservation.

Personal Story:

I have apologized to both of my sons for however they felt I hurt their feelings. Most of the time it wasn't about what I said, because my oldest son even admitted that it was the truth they needed to hear—but it was my tone. My response to that is this: if I have warned you about what I saw that you could not see, or advised you that the choices you were making were not the best choices, how exactly am I expected to say it—dripping with honey? Truth rarely tastes sweet.

And still, I showed accountability. I have been present for them both. I showed up, I supported, I stayed silent even when I didn't agree with their choices. With my younger son, the one I'm now estranged from, I gave even more of myself. But after the last curse word, the last threat, the last false narrative—I reached my breaking point. That was the day I made the decision to detach. Not out of lack of love, but out of love for myself. I will not sacrifice myself anymore.

Moving Forward

I didn't walk away because I stopped loving my son—I walked away because I finally started loving myself enough to protect my peace. Detachment, for me, became the line between survival and self-respect.

JOURNAL PROMPTS

What do I fear will happen if I detach?

How has holding on too tightly hurt me in the past?

What does healthy detachment look like for me now?

REFLECTION EXERCISE

Write a letter to yourself as if you were your best friend. Release the guilt tied to detaching. Affirm that your peace and your heart is worth protecting.

_____
_____
_____
_____
_____
_____
_____
_____
_____
_____
_____
_____
_____
_____
_____
_____

AFFIRMATION

"I can love without losing myself. Detachment protects my peace."

"Detachment isn't rejection—it's protection."

CHAPTER 3

Releasing the Need for Their Approval

One of the hardest things to accept is that your worth as a parent and a human being is not tied to your child's current opinion of you. If it was, then every act of love you gave them when they were young and since they became adults, wouldn't count unless they "approved" later. And we know that's not true.

Your Worth Does Not Expire Because Your Relationship Doesn't Reflect What Society Says

Now let me point out: some of your kids stopped talking to you because of your political choices and even when some of you say "they just stopped talking to me and I don't know why", you really do know why. And, although your worth as a good parent should not be based on your political choices, do know that dependent upon your political choices and views, their opinion and their perception of you may have definitely changed.

Some of you "parented" and they are now wrapping their entire identities up into trauma for having to do chores, having rules, curfews etc. Again, imperfect parenting is not necessarily bad parenting and again, your worth is not tied to them creating trauma narratives out of being parented with rules and expectations.

When Worth Gets Tied to Children's Opinions

As parents, many of us were conditioned to measure our value through how our children saw us. If they smiled and were happy all of the time or doted on us, we felt like good parents. If they rejected us or disrespected us or made bad decisions we carried it as failure. But worth that depends on another person's opinion—especially the opinion of a child navigating their own lives, their own experiences or even their own wounds—is unhealthy as hell. When your worth is tied to their shifting emotions, you're always one argument, one silent treatment, one false narrative away from feeling worthless. Your value cannot rest in the hands of anyone else let alone our children, it is not tied to them applauding you, giving you accolades, coming to Sunday dinner, spending holidays with you nor vacationing with you. So stop that shit immediately!

Breaking the "Performance Trap"

How many of you have been performing for the love of your child? I mean really roll back that beautiful bean footage in your mind how we jumped through hoops to be the cool parent who we just wanted our kids to hang with us? We may have acted out of character to fit in with them like some high school kid trying to be down with the popular kids and in some cases, made a complete fool of ourselves performing for their love, walking on eggshells and staying silent, knowing damn well some of us could cut a diamond with our words when someone disrespects us. We put on these performative, inauthentic performances for their love. But that performance trap tells you that love has to be earned. That if you cook enough meals, say

Moving Forward

the right words, stay quiet when disrespected, or bend yourself into the shape they want, you'll be accepted. But performing for acceptance is exhausting, and it never works. The goalpost keeps moving, and the applause never comes. At some point, you realize you're performing for an audience that refuses to clap. Freedom comes when you step off that stage and stop performing for approval. Be your authentic self for your own peace.

Reclaiming Self-Worth Outside the Parent Role

You were a whole person before you became a parent. That truth hasn't changed, even if estrangement or disrespect makes you feel like your identity was consumed up by motherhood or fatherhood. Reclaiming self-worth means reminding yourself: you are more than the parent of an adult child. You are creative, intelligent, resilient, loving, resourceful. Being a parent is part of your story, but it is not the totality of your worth. When you reclaim your self-worth outside the role, you take back your freedom to define yourself on your own terms.

> You were enough then. You are enough now.
> Even if they never say it.

Personal Story:

I recalled my younger son brought a girl to our home, she had this nasty attitude from the moment she met me, and didn't understand the relationship dynamic he and I had clearly, as it related to our humor, In gest after he said something snarky, I said "boy get out of my house" and she immediately grabbed her bag and said "let's go!" Normally I would have said, "girl calm down, it's not that serious and clearly you don't get our dynamic" but I said nothing to keep the peace. He knew I was

Moving Forward

joking but didn't clear it up with her. That same girl months later called me after they had a fight, and I was telling her to remove herself from the situation before it escalated further and to calm down because she was very upset. She in turn started yelling and saying disparaging things about my husband and I, cursed me out and then when I matched her energy this time around, threatened to send people to our home with guns. MY home where we have peace and don't engage with people like this. I realized right then that me performing and pretending to be someone I was not, to keep the peace would never happen again at the expense of my own peace. There are so many stories I could share where I was being performative to keep peace or to be loved by him and it did nothing but disturb my peace.

JOURNAL PROMPTS

In what ways have I allowed my children's opinions to define my worth as a parent and as a person?

_____
_____
_____
_____
_____
_____
_____
_____
_____
_____
_____
_____
_____
_____
_____
_____
_____
_____
_____

Where in my life am I still "performing" in hopes of being accepted, and what would freedom from that performance look like?

_____
_____
_____
_____
_____
_____
_____
_____
_____
_____
_____
_____
_____
_____
_____
_____
_____
_____
_____
_____
_____
_____

Who am I outside of my role as a parent—what qualities, gifts, and strengths define me on my own terms?

_____
_____
_____
_____
_____
_____
_____
_____
_____
_____
_____
_____
_____
_____
_____
_____
_____
_____
_____
_____
_____
_____

WRITE TWO LISTS

List A: *moments when you felt like your worth was only measured by your children's reactions, opinions, or approval.*

_____
_____
_____
_____
_____
_____
_____
_____
_____
_____
_____
_____
_____
_____
_____
_____
_____
_____
_____
_____

List B: *moments when you felt proud, accomplished, or whole completely outside of being a parent.*

Compare the two. Notice how many times your sense of worth came from your own strength, talents, and resilience. Keep this as a reminder that your identity extends beyond your role as "mom" or "dad."

_____
_____
_____
_____
_____
_____
_____
_____
_____
_____
_____
_____
_____
_____
_____
_____

AFFIRMATION

"My worth is not defined by their opinion. I am valuable, whole, and enough—outside of my role as a parent.

"Their approval is optional; your wholeness and identity outside of being a mom or dad is not."

CHAPTER 4

Protecting Your Peace
(Peace is the Boundary You Shouldn't Allow Anyone to Cross)

Choosing distance is sometimes the ultimate boundary. It says: *"I love you, but I will not allow your disrespect nor walk on eggshells any longer, keeping peace for others, but causing trauma within myself.*

Setting Unshakable Boundaries Without Explaining Yourself

Boundaries are non-negotiable for me now and don't need to be defended or justified—they need to be enforced. Too often, parents are pressured into giving a detailed explanation for every limit they set. But boundaries are not up for debate. A locked door doesn't explain why it's locked. It simply stays locked until the right key is present. Your peace deserves the same firmness. You don't owe anyone—especially those who have disrespected you—an explanation or long dissertation on why you are protecting yourself. Boundaries are about you, not them.

Moving Forward

Recognizing Manipulation & Guilt Tactics

Now get ready for the guilt tactics and the possible manipulation that may not just come from your child but may come from others on the outside looking in. Outsiders like: family members, friends who just don't understand your stand or situation or therapists that are telling parents "you should always be chasing your child". Girl Bye!

Manipulation often shows up as guilt: "You're supposed to be my mother." "If you loved me, you'd do this." "Other parents would…" These are traps meant to pull you back into compliance. Recognizing manipulation means naming it for what it is—a strategy to control your behavior. The moment you see guilt tactics for what they are, they lose their power. You don't have to argue. You don't have to defend yourself. You simply refuse to take the bait.

How to Stop Over-Explaining

Over-explaining is a survival strategy many parents pick up to avoid conflict. We think if we just explain clearly enough, they'll understand our perspective. But people committed to misunderstanding you will never "get it." Over-explaining drains your energy and invites more arguments. The truth is simple: "No" is a full sentence. Boundaries lose strength when they're wrapped in unnecessary explanations. Clarity is kindness—to yourself.

Personal Story

There came a point with my son where I realized I was explaining myself into exhaustion. Every boundary I set was met with emotional manipulation or straight-up disrespect. If I said "no," or "I am not responsible for your bad choices" he would

Moving Forward

continue to guilt trip me until it broke me down and I would cave. If I tried to stand firm, he would guilt-trip me. If I proved to him something he was saying was not true with facts and with proof, he would still believe and carry the lies he was telling about me and anyone else, to others. I found myself on this constant emotionally abusive roller coaster and I HATE roller coasters! I was constantly defending my right to peace, constantly trying to prove my love, constantly biting my tongue. Constantly doing everything BUT protecting peace nor myself!!

But no matter how many words I used, the response was the same: manipulation. I finally understood that I wasn't being asked for clarity—I was being baited into control. The more I explained, the more ammunition I gave him to push back. The last time it happened, after a heated exchange that left me drained, I stopped mid-sentence. I realized: I don't owe you an explanation for ANYTHING ANYMORE and in actuality never did. That was the moment I drew the line. No more over-explaining. No more defending myself nor my boundaries. I decided then that "no" would be enough.

I also had to set a hard boundary with my oldest son when he was losing his apartment. I have always talked to both sons about money management, how important having good credit was, even had them on my credit cards to help increase their scores. I gave him suggestions on how to manage his money to take care of his responsibilities where it wouldn't feel like such a burden and he didn't listen. Called him to come to a concert with us that I had gotten tickets for and he was in a panic because he was about to be evicted. He told me this and typically I would have asked "how much do you owe, I will help out or pay it to catch it up or you can come home." But not this time. I said "oh wow, well I hope it gets resolved." I hung up the phone, almost cried because I felt bad for him and because

Moving Forward

it was the hardest thing for me to not save him AGAIN! But he is over 30 years old, it was time for him to figure it out. I felt guilty but realized, his choices not to listen when I gave him solid advice and guidance, was on him not me!

Setting boundaries with our kids is never easy at first. I had to sit with the discomfort of being misunderstood for saying no. But practice makes perfect! Saying less was actually saying more. It was me finally showing up for myself in the same way I had always shown up for them. Hell I have even had to set boundaries with my grandson and I love that little guy beyond measure. LOL!

JOURNAL PROMPTS

Where in my life am I still giving explanations when I don't owe one?

What guilt tactics have I fallen for in the past, and how can I respond differently next time?

_____
_____
_____
_____
_____
_____
_____
_____
_____
_____
_____
_____
_____
_____
_____
_____
_____
_____
_____
_____

How would it feel to state a boundary without apologizing or over-explaining?

REFLECTION EXERCISE

Practice writing three boundary statements without adding justification. Example:

- "I will not be spoken to with disrespect."
- "I will not lend money."
- "I will not attend if I feel unsafe."

Read them out loud until they feel natural in your voice.

_____
_____
_____
_____
_____
_____
_____
_____
_____
_____
_____
_____
_____
_____
_____
_____

AFFIRMATION

"My peace is sacred. My boundaries need no explanation"

"My peace is the boundary I will never allow anyone else to cross."

CHAPTER 5

Choosing Not to Reconcile

Okay now for those of you not here yet, that's fine but we don't judge those of us who are choosing not to reconcile. I constantly battle with: To reconcile or not to reconcile. When I have those moments, something always confirms that NOT reconciling is the best decision for me at least for right now. Doesn't mean I don't love my son it just means that in this current state of my life, I am choosing not to chase reconciliation for my own mental well-being and I deserve to have the same peace he feels entitled to be able to disturb. Sometimes walking away can be just as healing as reconciling. Unconditional love doesn't mean self-sacrifice or constant tolerance of abuse.

Not every parent wants reconciliation—and that's valid and they should not be judged if that is their choice and this is where many parents wrestle with guilt, shame, or second-guessing their decision. If reconciliation means returning to abuse, manipulation, or humiliation, then reconciliation isn't healing, it's harm. You are allowed to choose peace instead and unapologetically.

To reach this decision, you often go through steps: accept reality, release guilt, define peace for yourself, build your new life, and protect the decision. Distance over disrespect is not selfishness—it's wisdom.

Closure may not come from reconciliation. It may come from you deciding you will no longer sacrifice your sanity, safety, or spirit. That decision is powerful.

When Reconciliation Harms

Some parents reach a point where reconciliation isn't healthy, safe, or even desired. And that's okay. Refusing reconciliation is not the absence of love—it is the presence of self-preservation. Let me repeat: Not every reconciliation is healthy. Returning to a relationship built on abuse, disrespect, or manipulation is not healing—it is harm. Choosing not to reconcile may be the bravest form of love you can show yourself.

Personal Story:

My son pushed me to set boundaries. Me choosing to set the strongest boundary I've ever set in my life was not about punishing him; it was about me being liberated and no longer accepting toxic behavior and abuse because he was my son. I had to prove to myself that love doesn't mean tolerating harm, and being a mom doesn't mean lifelong suffering.

I have been on the roller coaster of reconciliation with my son more times than I can count. The cycle was always the same: he would say the most damaging things to me, cause drama with outsiders that landed on our doorstep and put our safety in jeopardy, leave me stuck with the financial messes he caused, disappear for a few weeks or months, and then reappear as if nothing had ever happened and I would let it slide. It became a pattern of verbal abuse, emotional abuse,

Moving Forward

and financial abuse—followed by gaslighting. He would make me feel like I had no right to be hurt or upset, as if his readiness to speak again somehow erased the harm he had caused or erased the things he had said or done to me.

The truth is, some of the things he has said to me have cut deeper than anything I've heard from anyone else in my life. And the weight of that realization forced me to confront what I was truly accepting in the name of "having a "relationship" with my child." I would NEVER tolerate the shit he has said or done from anyone else but did because he is my son and society has brainwashed moms to tolerate this behavior because "it's your child". You should always be catering to them or chasing them right?

That was when I had to ask myself: Am I calling this reconciliation, or am I allowing cycles of abuse to continue? The difference between the two is everything, and seeing it clearly became the first step in choosing peace over proximity and distance over disrespect. It's been two years now as of September 2025 that I made this decision to be estranged and not seek reconciliation and I have unapologetic peace! And really don't give a damn what anyone on the outside that has not had my experience or doesn't understand as a mom, dad, friend, or stranger has to say about it.

Releasing the Guilt

Parents are told: we should always be there for your child no matter what, no matter how badly they treat you, no matter how you feel, no matter the emotional or even physical toll it takes on you.

Parents are told they should always hope, always wait, always keep the door open. But when reconciliation means

Moving Forward

losing yourself or jeopardizing your peace or emotional and physical wellbeing, the guilt of closing that door has to be released. You are not failing—you are choosing survival.

Some Steps to Getting There

1. Accept Reality – Acknowledge that having your child in your life in this moment may not be healthy for you or them.

2. Release Guilt – Let go of the pressure to "always keep the door open." Ignore what ANY outsiders have to say about your choice.

3. Define Peace for Yourself – Decide what healing looks like without their involvement.

4. Protect the Decision – Remind yourself: sometimes the most important choices are choosing distance over disrespect and peace over proximity and it is not selfishness—it's self-preservation.

JOURNAL PROMPTS

What would reconciliation cost me right now?

What patterns am I unwilling to re-enter?

How does choosing distance affirm my value and peace?

REFLECTION EXERCISE

Write a release letter to the idea of reconciliation. Acknowledge why it is not the healthiest choice for you now and release the guilt connected to this decision.

_____
_____
_____
_____
_____
_____
_____
_____
_____
_____
_____
_____
_____
_____
_____
_____
_____

AFFIRMATION

"Walking away protects my peace. It is an act of love, not failure."

"Sometimes the bravest love is walking away."

CHAPTER 6

Blood Doesn't Always Guarantee Love

The Assumption of Blood

As parents, many of us believed that because we gave life, sacrificed, and loved unconditionally, the bond of blood would guarantee respect and love in return from our children. We assumed biology meant unconditional love from our kids. That's why estrangement feels so damn weird and unnatural—it dismantles everything we believed about parenthood and that's why so many of you are struggling even when it's been 5 or more years in estrangement.

The Real Tea

Biology alone will not make another person love, respect, or cherish you. Estrangement proves that unconditional love on your part does not always guarantee unconditional love back. That truth cuts deeply—but it is not proof of your failure. It just proves that blood does not override choice and isn't always thicker than water.

Moving Forward

Honor the Children Who Do Show Up

While we grieve estrangement, it is important not to overlook the children who remain loving, respectful, and present. I said this in Chapter 11 of my book "Reclaiming Your Identity". They deserve more than to become emotional stand-ins for the sibling who is absent. Honor them, love them freely—but resist the urge to smother or become codependent. Their presence is a blessing, not a crutch. Allow them to thrive without carrying the weight of your mourning. So, if you have found yourself doing this, it's time for you to have a conversation with the kid(s), this applies to, asking for their forgiveness and letting them know that you see them!

When You Have One Child

This comes up often, and I see some of you say "but I only have one child". For parents who have only one child, estrangement can feel like a total loss. In those moments, it's easy to believe your love has nowhere else to go. But love doesn't expire because one relationship is broken. You can choose to redirect that love into other connections—nieces, nephews, children in your community, or those who've lost their parents and need guidance. You can join support groups where your experience creates empathy and strength for others. Shifting your focus this way reminds you: while reconciliation may feel far off, love still has places to live and you still have love to give.

Shifting Focus Without Losing Love

Shifting your focus away from estrangement doesn't mean you've stopped loving your child. It means you refuse to let their choices consume your life. It means you are committed to finding peace, joy, and purpose—whether reconciliation happens or not.

AFFIRMATION

"I will not let estrangement blind me to the love that still surrounds me. My love has room to grow, to heal, and to live beyond one broken bond."

"Family is who shows up, not just who shares your blood."

CHAPTER 7

Reclaiming Joy (Finding Joy in the Life You Still Have)

Joy as Rebellion

Estrangement can drain your joy, but if you want to piss your kid off... reclaim your joy as your rebellion against the pain, the disrespect and emotional manipulation and control. Every smile, every laugh, every moment of delight is proof that your life is not defined by loss. Joy is not denial that this doesn't hurt—it is survival. And to be honest, finding your joy isn't even about them, it's really about you!

Finding Joy in the Small Things

Joy doesn't have to be grand. It begins in the small things—a walk, a favorite song, dancing around the house like you did when you were a teenager, sitting and sipping on your favorite cup of tea, coffee or some really good wine! Even a good whiskey or brandy if that's your drink of choice. It's whatever YOU choose to do. These moments rebuild your spirit, one step at a time. Girl wake up, crank up some music and dance while you are getting dressed or around the house cleaning, start having date nights and enjoying your partner and again... REST!!

Joy Without Guilt

You do not owe your suffering to anyone. Some of these kids that have become estranged or who have been abusive want to control your emotions. That's why they are trolling in safe spaces where parents are finding support or healing. That is why they are following you on social media trying to keep tabs on what you are doing and when they see your sad posts or you are begging them to reconcile or they see or hear how bad you are looking physically, or someone tells them how sad you are, THEY are the ones getting the joy! Snap out of it! Reclaiming joy does not mean you love your child less—it means you refuse to let pain steal your life. YOU ARE ENTITLED TO JOY!!

Personal Story

I started doing things to find my joy like traveling, or something as simple as resting. We often take rest for granted and it's needed if for nothing else: to reset our nervous systems from all of the anxiety and emotional pain we have been through. Hell I just started living more for me and that alone has brought me joy!

JOURNAL PROMPTS

What activities bring me joy regardless of circumstances?

How have I silenced my own joy out of guilt?

What small joy can I commit to this week?

REFLECTION EXERCISE

Create a 'Joy Inventory.' List 10 things, no matter how small, that bring you joy. Commit to one this week.

_____
_____
_____
_____
_____
_____
_____
_____
_____
_____
_____
_____
_____
_____
_____
_____
_____
_____
_____
_____

AFFIRMATION

*"My joy is mine to reclaim.
I refuse to surrender it to pain."*

"Joy is my rebellion against pain and it's not petty, it's for ME!"

CHAPTER 8

Writing a New Chapter for Yourself (Reclaiming Your Identity)

Waiting keeps you stuck in limbo. Every day spent wondering if they'll come back is a day you aren't fully living. Visualizing your future without the weight of waiting doesn't mean you've stopped loving your child—it means you refuse to let uncertainty hold your life hostage. Take a moment to imagine: What does your life look like if you stop waiting? What dreams, hobbies, or goals have been on hold? What would it feel like to step back into joy without the shadow of estrangement dictating your every move?

When you give yourself permission to envision a future beyond waiting, you open the door to healing and possibility. The future is not an empty space—it is your canvas.

Creating a Personal Peace Plan

Peace doesn't arrive by accident; it has to be intentional. A personal peace plan is your roadmap for moving forward. It might include practices like journaling, therapy, prayer, meditation, setting stricter boundaries, or even cultivating new friendships. It can be as simple as committing to one joyful activity each week or as structured as writing out your goals for

Moving Forward

the next year. In fact, I am challenging you to find one thing at minimum that you can do to enjoy your life, snap out of that depression and have some fun!

The point is to create a framework that helps you protect your peace daily. Think of it as building a safety net—something that holds you up when the weight of estrangement tries to pull you back down. Because trust me: I too understand how those thoughts creep up because they are always lurking. The moment you feel it coming up, ctrl+alt+delete. Shift that thought immediately. And if that thought brings up emotions you just cannot shake, ride it out and cry, scream or whatever you need to do to move THROUGH it!

How to Keep Healing Forward

Healing forward means you keep walking, even with the heartbreak or the longing to reconcile. It's understanding that moving on doesn't erase your love for your child. I feel like I have to reiterate this statement several times for you to get it. It doesn't mean you've cut them out of your heart—it means you've chosen not to sacrifice your entire life waiting for something that may never come.

You can love your child and still love yourself enough to move forward. You can hold hope for reconciliation without holding yourself hostage to it. Healing forward is not betrayal; it is survival. And with each step, you prove that peace is possible—right here, right now.

That's why I wrote *Reclaiming Your Identity*. Because so many of us lose ourselves in the chaos of estrangement, disrespect, and abuse, and we forget that our lives still have meaning outside of this pain. This book, *Moving Forward*, is the

Moving Forward

continuation of that journey—helping you not only reclaim who you are, but also move forward into the peace you deserve.

Personal Story:

There was a moment when I realized I had been holding my life hostage, and blaming myself for everything that went wrong with my sons. I started sitting cozy in the mentality that my joy, my healing, my peace, my happiness was contingent only upon their successes or their validation of me. I paused my aspirations for them, I sacrificed things I wanted or needed for them even as adults as if it was my duty to do so no matter how I was treated or spoken to. Had I not made the decision to become estranged and not spend my life focusing on reconciliation, I would have even been putting my future on pause, all because I was expecting as a mom for my son to love me as much as I did him or for him to treat me with the respect I deserve! September 15, 2023 was the day it hit me: I was losing years of my life waiting for someone else to change, when it was me that needed to make this change all along. I lost who I was and tolerated far more than I should have, mother or not.

That's why I wrote Reclaiming Your Identity. Because so many of us lose ourselves in this cycle, and we need to remember who we are outside of it. For me, writing that book was the first step in saying: My identity would no longer be tied to his false narratives, his manipulation or him not loving me the way I thought a child should love their parents. I didn't need his validation or his brother's to KNOW who I am as a mom and have always been. The only difference was that I was now setting boundaries and no longer trying to fix those things I didn't break. Moving forward didn't mean I stopped loving my child. It meant I finally loved myself enough to stop sacrificing my life in the process.

JOURNAL PROMPTS

What parts of my life have I put on hold because I was waiting for reconciliation?

What three practices could I add to my personal peace plan today?

How can I remind myself daily that moving forward doesn't mean I've stopped loving my child?

REFLECTION EXERCISE

Write a one-page vision of your life one year from now—without factoring in reconciliation. Focus only on your peace, your joy, and your goals. Be specific: what are you doing, where are you, who is supporting you? Read it back to yourself whenever you feel pulled back into waiting.

_____
_____
_____
_____
_____
_____
_____
_____
_____
_____
_____
_____
_____
_____
_____
_____
_____
_____

AFFIRMATION

"I will not wait in silence for my life to begin. I move forward in peace, while keeping love in my heart."

"I deserve far more than watching time go by, wasting my energy in heartbreak, waiting on reconciliation."

CHAPTER 9

Navigating Reconciliation if Your Child Returns

Reconciliation can feel like the answer to every prayer—but it must be handled with caution. I even did a podcast episode on this: My Child Reached Out To Me, Now What?!" I discussed that if your child does reach out to you or is finally open to reconciliation, proceed with extreme caution and guard your heart, emotions and your wallet.

Don't act super thirsty or super excited until you evaluate they "why and the what". The: why now, the why are they reaching out now, what changed, what do they want all of a sudden, and is this to really reconcile or to gain control of my emotions all over again and then they are gone again. So again, proceed with caution.

Just because your child returns doesn't mean the wounds their absence caused or hurtful things said disappear. Healing takes time, accountability, and trust on both sides. Enter reconciliation with open eyes, not just elation and blind hope.

If you've done the work to heal, don't abandon it the moment they return. Stay grounded in your boundaries, your peace practices, and your self-respect. Reconciliation should not erase the progress you've made—it should build on it. You

Moving Forward

will not be the same parent you were before and they will have to decide if they can accept that new you or not.

It's also normal to feel anxious or even 'gun shy' when they come back. You're afraid of being hurt again. To protect yourself, set clear expectations: name your non-negotiables (respect, honesty, safety), move slowly, and seek mutual accountability. If you've already owned your part, don't keep apologizing.

CHAPTER 10

Grandparents Bring It On In

For grandparents, reconciliation often feels tied to the hope of keeping a relationship with the grandchildren. Many of you have walked on eggshells, tolerated disrespect, and swallowed pain just for the chance to see them. But reconciliation that forces you to erase yourself isn't reconciliation—it's captivity. Access without respect is not peace.

Walking on Eggshells for Access

So many grandparents find themselves walking on eggshells—tolerating disrespect from their adult children—just for the chance to see their grandchildren. Every conversation feels like a test. Every boundary feels like a risk. You bite your tongue, accept treatment you'd never tolerate from anyone else, and pray that this "good behavior" will buy you access. But walking on eggshells is not family—it's survival mode. It leaves you anxious, depleted, and silenced.

Grandchildren See More Than You Think

Let me lean and whisper in your ear: your grandchildren notice more than anyone gives them credit for. They see the tension. They hear the words, even when whispered. They pick up on

Moving Forward

the way their parents speak about you—or don't speak about you at all. Children are incredibly perceptive, and while they may not fully understand what's happening, they can sense when love is being blocked or manipulated.

This is why it's so important for you to stay grounded in dignity and peace. Even if you have limited contact, your grandchildren will remember how you carried yourself. They will recall your kindness, your consistency, and your strength. They may not be able to challenge their parents now, but as they grow older, they will form their own opinions about the way relationships were handled. And your presence—even from a distance—can still plant seeds of truth and resilience in them. Keep those memory boxes I have suggested you start putting together on my lives and when they come looking for answers, you don't have to bash their parents. Hell, you don't even have to mention them. Just hand them the memory box and pick up from there.

Personal Story

I was sitting in the airport coming back from vacation and a woman was sitting across from me with a child in stroller He was about 4, with a pacifier in his mouth and a cellphone in his hand. I normally don't watch people but she caught and held my attention while waiting to board my flight. She didn't say a word, she looked anxious and it I could feel it. The child was falling asleep and his phone was sliding off of his lap, she picked it up, he woke up and started throwing a tantrum. He tossed that pacifier about 3 times, still not a word from her, just silence. He then got ready to toss his phone on the floor and a young lady came over to them. She told him not to throw the phone very sternly as she should have but the older woman, in which now I realized was the grandmother, still not a word! The

Moving Forward

child's mom is now chastising the grandmother and again, silence. What that told me in that moment was this woman was always walking on eggshells with the mom and that child. That she would always be silent because her proximity and access to this grandchild was even more important than her dignity. It made me sad for her. I hope she finds her voice at some point.

Pining for Reconciliation Through the Grandkids

For many grandparents, reconciliation becomes tangled up with the hope of maintaining a relationship with the grandkids. You tolerate abuse or manipulation because you don't want the children to lose you, too. You tell yourself, "If I can just keep the peace, if I can just stay close, maybe things will get better." But this cycle often keeps you trapped in heartbreak. Reconciliation based on desperation rarely creates true healing.

When the Hope Consumes You

Hoping for reconciliation is natural. But when that hope consumes your life, it robs you of the very joy your grandchildren should bring you. You find yourself constantly mourning, ruminating, and replaying arguments instead of enjoying the moments you do have. You start believing that unless reconciliation happens, your life has no peace. The truth? You can love your grandchildren deeply without sacrificing yourself to a toxic cycle.

Choosing Peace as a Grandparent

It's not easy. But at some point, you have to ask: Am I modeling strength and peace for my grandchildren, or am I showing them how to tolerate disrespect? Your grandkids don't need a

Moving Forward

broken version of you. They need to see resilience. They need to see that love doesn't mean erasing yourself. Choosing peace—even if it means limited access—shows them what true self-respect looks like.

Always Remember This

Do not forget that your life is still your own. Being a grandparent is a gift, but it is not your entire identity. Pour into friendships, community, hobbies, faith, or causes that bring you joy. The more you fill yourself up with peace and purpose, the less you'll feel consumed by the pain of what's missing.

JOURNAL PROMPTS

In what ways have I walked on eggshells just to keep access to my grandkids?

_____
_____
_____
_____
_____
_____
_____
_____
_____
_____
_____
_____
_____
_____
_____
_____
_____
_____
_____

How has my hope for reconciliation consumed me emotionally or spiritually?

What would it look like to love my grandchildren and protect my peace at the same time?

AFFIRMATION

"I will not walk on eggshells to prove my love. I can be a grandparent with peace, dignity, and strength."

CLOSING

Your Peace Is Sacred

Whether reconciliation happens or not, whether you are choosing to wait for it to happen or you have chosen to move forward just know this: If reconciliation comes, let it meet you in a place of peace, healing and empowerment. If it never comes, let your peace carry you anyway, to move forward with some ease.

Your worth, your identity, your future—it was never dependent on your child's validation of you, being estranged, tolerating abuse or waiting for their apology. You are not weak for loving your child. You are not a failure nor are you selfish for protecting yourself.

Your peace is well deserved and non-negotiable. Claim it, protect it, and live it.

ACKNOWLEDGMENTS

First, to the parents who have trusted me with your stories, your pain, and your truth. Having the courage to speak up and say what so many parents are ashamed and afraid to say has not been easy.

But I will continue to speak truth unapologetically about this epidemic and the change in how most aspects of parenting are now viewed as toxic or traumatic, when in most cases that's simply not true. I will keep holding space for those that felt like they were alone and now realize they are not and this is happening around the world.

This book carries all our voices.

To the mothers and fathers who are quietly navigating estrangement and disrespect. Thank you for reminding me that even in silence, there is strength.

To my community, the listeners of the *Mum's True Tea Podcast*, and those who read my first book, *Reclaiming Your Identity*—your feedback, encouragement, and honesty pushed me to write this one. You've made me believe that telling the raw truth heals more than hiding it ever could.

Finally, to those who have stood beside me in my personal life, especially my amazing husband—the one who loves me without conditions, who honors and supports my dreams, as do I with his, and who reminds me I am Superwoman even in my weakest moments.

Thank you for being the proof that love and respect can exist together.

YOUR HEALING DOESN'T END HERE

If this book has spoken to your heart, I want you to know you don't have to walk this journey alone.

I created the **Healing & Empowered Reset** — a 5-week group coaching program for mothers ready to:

- Stop suffering in silence
- Reclaim peace and identity
- Heal even without reconciliation

Your next step is waiting.

Scan the QR code below or visit **MumsTrueTea.com/coaching** to join us.

With love and truth,

Kendall L. Williams
Founder, *Mum's True Tea*

www.ingramcontent.com/pod-product-compliance
Lightning Source LLC
Chambersburg PA
CBHW070321100426
42743CB00011B/2513